PRACTICE & PROGRESS

Lesson Notebook

Assignment and Evaluation Record

By

Carolyn Inabinet and Paula Peterson-Heil

with

NANCY & RANDALL FABER

_____

STUDENT NAME

PIANO ADVENTURES®

Production: Frank and Gail Hackinson / Production Coordinator: Marilyn Cole / Design: Gwen Terpstra

A Note . . .

to the Student:

Congratulations on your commitment to music lessons! The Lesson Notebook is designed to aid your progress and to help you, your parents, and your teacher have a better understanding of each other as you work together toward your music goals.

Have you heard the story of the three students and the apple? A teacher gave an apple to each of the three students. Their assignment was simple: eat the apple. The first student was an eager beaver. He attempted to do this task very quickly, trying to put the whole apple into his mouth at one time. The second student had a different idea. Her solution was to first peel the apple. This took her some time and she never got around to taking one bite.

The third student decided to take one bite of the apple, chew thoroughly, and swallow. Then take another bite, and another – until the whole apple was gone. She did not try to do something impossible like the first student, and she did not waste time like the second student. This last approach is highly recommended for your success as a music student.

Does your teacher at school give you homework? Your teacher may give you an English assignment to bring home. You complete the assignment that evening and take it to school the next morning. As a music student, however, you bring home an assignment that is to be finished in one *week*. How can you best organize that weekly assignment? You don't want to be like the eager beaver and attempt an impossible task, or be like the student who wastes time and accomplishes nothing.

As you use this notebook, you will learn to play your musical instrument the way the third student ate her apple: one bite at a time. This notebook will help you and your teacher define those "bites of apples" (the goals to accomplish with each piece). Like the third student described, you will be successful in your practice. You will learn music step by step as you accomplish each goal your teacher writes in your *Practice & Progress* notebook. Over time, you will have made significant progress.

Enjoy your road to success, and remember how to practice for progress: organize a big assignment into smaller parts.

to the Parent:

As a music student, your son or daughter brings home a weekly assignment that consists of different elements. There are new pieces to be learned, pieces to be memorized, pieces with a challenging section to be mastered, technical exercises, written work, etc. How does your child organize this weekly assignment into a daily practice session? How involved are you in helping with this organization?

This Lesson Notebook is designed to increase communication among student, teacher, and parent. Its purpose is three-fold:

(1) to record daily practice each week

(2) to define specific practice goals

(3) to provide a weekly progress report for the parent and student

It is your responsibility to sign the practice schedule provided on the Practice Plan pages. The teacher will record the lesson grade and complete the Weekly Summary charts printed on the inside covers. You will be able to see at a glance how your child is progressing from week to week.

You now have at your fingertips a very specific way to help your child organize a practice session. As a parent, you can be most effective by reading each assignment and reinforcing those goals that the teacher has set out to accomplish during the week. Ask your child questions; help decide which goal(s) to accomplish per session; ask which goals are easy and which are hard. Be specific in your questions. Rather than ask, "Did you practice 30 minutes?", ask, "Did you memorize the first part of . . . . ?" If your child practices long enough to accomplish X number of goals per session rather than just spending 30 minutes practicing, success will be evident. A sense of accomplishment will dominate the practice session. Even if only one goal is completed, that sense of accomplishment will be more constructive than 30 minutes of merely playing through pieces.

Good practice habits with music study will positively affect any long-term project that involves a series of tasks. Your child can learn how to organize time effectively, accomplish specific goals, and feel successful. Isn't it wonderful that music lessons can offer so much?

ISBN 978-1-61677-024-2

A Note to the Teacher:

Practice & Progress is designed to increase communication among student, teacher, and parent. Three ingredients are essential for successful practice:

- time commitment
- organized practice
- evaluation

Practice & Progress is a useful tool that allows student, teacher, and parent to hear and see the *quality* and *quantity* of practice on a weekly basis. The booklet is to be used for a full calendar year – 43 Practice Plan pages allow for summer study.

Success is the key for productive students. How do we foster success at home? How do we help parents and students during those six days away from the weekly lessons? As teachers, we need to be specific in our expectations and provide our students with feedback on their achievement of those expectations.

Time Commitment

Practice & Progress provides a written Practice Agreement which should be read and completed by both student and parent(s). This agreement contains specific suggestions for a weekly practice goal. Success in accomplishing this weekly practice goal is recorded in the Practice Plan pages, as well as on the weekly Summary charts printed on the inside covers.

Practice Plan

The Practice Plan assignment pages provide room for the teacher to define specific goals. Each written goal should be concise for ease of understanding. A typical goal for a new piece could be: "learn right hand notes and fingering." It is important to consistently reinforce the idea that practice time is an opportunity to accomplish goals. A feeling of success will then motivate your students to return to practice the following day.

When we can be precise in defining each goal for an assignment, students and parents can structure practice sessions that will result in improvement. Clear and specific teacher expectations will result in more effective practice at home.

Evaluation

Practice & Progress provides students and parents with feedback, an element often overlooked in the private music lesson. Each practice goal is graded, and the overall lesson grade is recorded on the Practice Plan and on the Weekly Summary chart. With a grading scale of *outstanding, excellent, satisfactory, improving,* and *needs work,* no message of failure is conveyed.

Practice & Progress provides a thorough summary of the student's progress at a glance. The Practice Time/Award and Lesson Grade on the Weekly Summary chart provide the student, teacher, and parents a concise view of the quantity of practice and the quality of the lesson. A Repertoire list and a Technique chart further assist the teacher in tracking the student's progress.

How to use *Practice & Progress*

1. Students and parents read the Practice Agreement and the foreword. They complete and sign the Practice Agreement which commits students to a specific weekly practice time.

2. The teacher enters the lesson assignment and specific practice goals on the Practice Plan page.

3. Students and parents record the practice time on the daily log provided on the Practice Plan page as the student practices the lesson at home. Parents sign the Practice Plan page before each weekly lesson.

4. The teacher checks the practice time for the week and writes the practice time on the Weekly Summary (inside covers). As an alternative, the teacher may wish to place a sticker in this practice entry when the student has met the weekly practice goal.

5. The teacher grades each lesson goal as the lesson progresses and gives a comprehensive lesson grade. This is entered on the Practice Plan page and the Weekly Summary chart.

6. The teacher records memorized, or completed selections on the repertoire page and technical skills on the Technique chart. (These are located in the back of the book.)

Awards

An award system can easily be used in conjunction with *Practice & Progress*. A *suggested* award system for practice time is:

- A sticker placed on the Weekly Summary chart indicates the student has met the weekly practice goal.

- A star indicates the goal was achieved without a parent's reminder to practice.

A teacher may wish to implement a system of his/her own. Annual or semester awards, such as trophies, ribbons, musical gifts, etc., can also be used. *Practice & Progress* makes the record keeping easy.

PRACTICE AGREEMENT

This Practice Agreement is made between students and parents. Students need to be aware of the necessity of practice and the need to set aside time each day for *uninterrupted* practice. Parents of students from kindergarten through eighth grade need to follow through by recording practice times and signing practice schedules. High school students should also make a commitment to a weekly practice routine. Each weekly assignment will be graded and practice times will be recorded beginning the week of _____.

Guidelines for Practice

Students will determine their weekly time commitment within a suggested framework.

Levels 1-3: 20+ minutes five times per week *minimum.*

Level 4 and above: 30+ minutes five times per week *minimum.*

Students will progress faster if they choose more practice time.

The written practice record allows the teacher to evaluate whether the assignment is too difficult or insufficiently practiced. If a student consistently practices less than the time agreed to in this Practice Agreement, a four-week evaluation period will be set for parent(s), student, and teacher to work out a solution. Students and parents are invited to call and discuss problems or concerns. Parents are encouraged to be actively involved by discussing the weekly practice goals and taking time to listen to their children practice.

Goals and Grades

Both teachers and students are encouraged to define practice goals. A feeling of success is essential when practicing. Therefore, practice time should be spent working towards a specific goal with each piece, rather than simply playing through assigned pieces. The lesson grade is then based on the achievement of these specific goals.

I, _____ agree to practice _____ minutes a day, five days a week.

_____   _____
Student   Parent(s)

PRACTICE PLAN

Comments ▼

Grade ▼

| O = Outstanding |
| E = Excellent |
| S = Satisfactory |
| I = Improving |
| N = Needs work |

Date ▶

Goal	Day 1	2	3	4	5	6	7	Total	Parent Signature

Grade	Technique/Theory	Practice Goals

Grade	Repertoire	Practice Goals

FF1024

PRACTICE PLAN

Comments ▼

Grade ▼

Date ▶

Goal	Day 1	2	3	4	5	6	7	Total	Parent Signature

Grade	Technique/Theory	Practice Goals

Grade	Repertoire	Practice Goals

FF1024

PRACTICE PLAN

Comments ▼

Grade ▼

Date ▶

Goal	Day 1	2	3	4	5	6	7	Total	Parent Signature

Grade	Technique/Theory	Practice Goals

Grade	Repertoire	Practice Goals

FF1024

PRACTICE PLAN

Comments ▼

Grade ▼

O = Outstanding
E = Excellent
S = Satisfactory
I = Improving
N = Needs work

Date ▶

Goal	Day 1	2	3	4	5	6	7	Total	Parent Signature

Grade	Technique/Theory	Practice Goals

Grade	Repertoire	Practice Goals

FF1024

PRACTICE PLAN

Comments ▼

Grade ▼

| O = Outstanding |
| E = Excellent |
| S = Satisfactory |
| I = Improving |
| N = Needs work |

Date ▶

Goal	Day 1	2	3	4	5	6	7	Total	Parent Signature

Grade	Technique/Theory	Practice Goals

Grade	Repertoire	Practice Goals

FF1024

PRACTICE PLAN

Comments ▼

Grade ▼

| O = Outstanding |
| E = Excellent |
| S = Satisfactory |
| I = Improving |
| N = Needs work |

Date ▶

Goal	Day 1	2	3	4	5	6	7	Total	Parent Signature

Grade	Technique/Theory	Practice Goals

Grade	Repertoire	Practice Goals

PRACTICE PLAN

Comments ▼

Grade ▼

| O = Outstanding |
| E = Excellent |
| S = Satisfactory |
| I = Improving |
| N = Needs work |

Date ▶

Goal	Day 1	2	3	4	5	6	7	Total	Parent Signature

Grade	Technique/Theory	Practice Goals

Grade	Repertoire	Practice Goals

FF1024

PRACTICE PLAN

Comments ▼

Grade ▼

Date ▶

Goal	Day 1	2	3	4	5	6	7	Total	Parent Signature

Grade	Technique/Theory	Practice Goals

Grade	Repertoire	Practice Goals

FF1024

PRACTICE PLAN

Comments ▼

Grade ▼

O = Outstanding
E = Excellent
S = Satisfactory
I = Improving
N = Needs work

Date ▶

Goal	Day 1	2	3	4	5	6	7	Total	Parent Signature

Grade	Technique/Theory	Practice Goals

Grade	Repertoire	Practice Goals

FF1024

PRACTICE PLAN

Comments ▼

Grade ▼

Date ▶

Goal	Day 1	2	3	4	5	6	7	Total	Parent Signature

Grade	Technique/Theory	Practice Goals

Grade	Repertoire	Practice Goals

FF1024

PRACTICE PLAN

Comments ▼

Grade ▼

| O = Outstanding |
| E = Excellent |
| S = Satisfactory |
| I = Improving |
| N = Needs work |

Date ▶

Goal	Day 1	2	3	4	5	6	7	Total	Parent Signature

Grade	Technique/Theory	Practice Goals

Grade	Repertoire	Practice Goals

FF1024

PRACTICE PLAN

Comments ▼

Grade ▼

Date ▶

O = Outstanding
E = Excellent
S = Satisfactory
I = Improving
N = Needs work

Goal	Day 1	2	3	4	5	6	7	Total	Parent Signature

Grade	Technique/Theory	Practice Goals

Grade	Repertoire	Practice Goals

FF1024

PRACTICE PLAN

Comments ▼

Grade ▼

| O = Outstanding |
| E = Excellent |
| S = Satisfactory |
| I = Improving |
| N = Needs work |

Date ▶

Goal	Day 1	2	3	4	5	6	7	Total	Parent Signature

Grade	Technique/Theory	Practice Goals

Grade	Repertoire	Practice Goals

FF1024

PRACTICE PLAN

Comments ▼

Grade ▼

| O = Outstanding |
| E = Excellent |
| S = Satisfactory |
| I = Improving |
| N = Needs work |

Date ▶

Goal	Day 1	2	3	4	5	6	7	Total	Parent Signature

Grade	Technique/Theory	Practice Goals

Grade	Repertoire	Practice Goals

FF1024

PRACTICE PLAN

Comments ▼

Grade ▼

| O = Outstanding |
| E = Excellent |
| S = Satisfactory |
| I = Improving |
| N = Needs work |

Date ▶

Goal	Day 1	2	3	4	5	6	7	Total	Parent Signature

Grade	Technique/Theory	Practice Goals

Grade	Repertoire	Practice Goals

FF1024

PRACTICE PLAN

Comments ▼

Grade ▼

Date ▶

O	= Outstanding
E	= Excellent
S	= Satisfactory
I	= Improving
N	= Needs work

Goal	Day 1	2	3	4	5	6	7	Total	Parent Signature

Grade	Technique/Theory	Practice Goals

Grade	Repertoire	Practice Goals

FF1024

PRACTICE PLAN

Comments ▼

Grade ▼

O	= Outstanding
E	= Excellent
S	= Satisfactory
I	= Improving
N	= Needs work

Date ▶

Goal	Day 1	2	3	4	5	6	7	Total	Parent Signature

Grade	Technique/Theory	Practice Goals

Grade	Repertoire	Practice Goals

FF1024

PRACTICE PLAN

Comments ▼

Grade ▼

O = Outstanding
E = Excellent
S = Satisfactory
I = Improving
N = Needs work

Date ▶

Goal	Day 1	2	3	4	5	6	7	Total	Parent Signature

Grade	Technique/Theory	Practice Goals

Grade	Repertoire	Practice Goals

FF1024

PRACTICE PLAN

Comments ▼

Grade ▼

O = Outstanding
E = Excellent
S = Satisfactory
I = Improving
N = Needs work

Date ▶

Goal	Day 1	2	3	4	5	6	7	Total	Parent Signature

Grade	Technique/Theory	Practice Goals

Grade	Repertoire	Practice Goals

FF1024

PRACTICE PLAN

Comments ▼

Grade ▼

Date ▶

O = Outstanding
E = Excellent
S = Satisfactory
I = Improving
N = Needs work

Goal	Day 1	2	3	4	5	6	7	Total	Parent Signature

Grade	Technique/Theory	Practice Goals

Grade	Repertoire	Practice Goals

PRACTICE PLAN

Comments ▼

Grade ▼

| O = Outstanding |
| E = Excellent |
| S = Satisfactory |
| I = Improving |
| N = Needs work |

Date ▶

Goal	Day 1	2	3	4	5	6	7	Total	Parent Signature

Grade	Technique/Theory	Practice Goals

Grade	Repertoire	Practice Goals

FF1024

PRACTICE PLAN

Comments ▼

Grade ▼

O = Outstanding
E = Excellent
S = Satisfactory
I = Improving
N = Needs work

Date ▶

Goal	Day 1	2	3	4	5	6	7	Total	Parent Signature

Grade	Technique/Theory	Practice Goals

Grade	Repertoire	Practice Goals

FF1024

PRACTICE PLAN

Comments ▼

Grade ▼

O = Outstanding
E = Excellent
S = Satisfactory
I = Improving
N = Needs work

Date ▶

Goal	Day 1	2	3	4	5	6	7	Total	Parent Signature

Grade	Technique/Theory	Practice Goals

Grade	Repertoire	Practice Goals

FF1024

PRACTICE PLAN

Comments ▼

Grade ▼

Date ▶

Goal	Day 1	2	3	4	5	6	7	Total	Parent Signature

Grade	Technique/Theory	Practice Goals

Grade	Repertoire	Practice Goals

FF1024

PRACTICE PLAN

Comments ▼

Grade ▼

O = Outstanding
E = Excellent
S = Satisfactory
I = Improving
N = Needs work

Date ▶

Goal	Day 1	2	3	4	5	6	7	Total	Parent Signature

Grade	Technique/Theory	Practice Goals

Grade	Repertoire	Practice Goals

FF1024

PRACTICE PLAN

Comments ▼

Grade ▼

O = Outstanding
E = Excellent
S = Satisfactory
I = Improving
N = Needs work

Date ▶

Goal	Day 1	2	3	4	5	6	7	Total	Parent Signature

Grade	Technique/Theory	Practice Goals

Grade	Repertoire	Practice Goals

FF1024

PRACTICE PLAN

Comments ▼

Grade ▼

| O = Outstanding |
| E = Excellent |
| S = Satisfactory |
| I = Improving |
| N = Needs work |

Date ▶

Goal	Day 1	2	3	4	5	6	7	Total	Parent Signature

Grade	Technique/Theory	Practice Goals

Grade	Repertoire	Practice Goals

FF1024

PRACTICE PLAN

Comments ▼

Grade ▼

O = Outstanding
E = Excellent
S = Satisfactory
I = Improving
N = Needs work

Date ▶

Goal	Day 1	2	3	4	5	6	7	Total	Parent Signature

Grade	Technique/Theory	Practice Goals

Grade	Repertoire	Practice Goals

FF1024

PRACTICE PLAN

Comments ▼

Grade ▼

| O = Outstanding |
| E = Excellent |
| S = Satisfactory |
| I = Improving |
| N = Needs work |

Date ▶

Goal	Day 1	2	3	4	5	6	7	Total	Parent Signature

Grade	Technique/Theory	Practice Goals

Grade	Repertoire	Practice Goals

FF1024

PRACTICE PLAN

Comments ▼

Grade ▼

O = Outstanding
E = Excellent
S = Satisfactory
I = Improving
N = Needs work

Date ▶

Goal	Day 1	2	3	4	5	6	7	Total	Parent Signature

Grade	Technique/Theory	Practice Goals

Grade	Repertoire	Practice Goals

FF1024

PRACTICE PLAN

Comments ▼

Grade ▼

O = Outstanding
E = Excellent
S = Satisfactory
I = Improving
N = Needs work

Date ▶

Goal	Day 1	2	3	4	5	6	7	Total	Parent Signature

Grade	Technique/Theory	Practice Goals

Grade	Repertoire	Practice Goals

FF1024

PRACTICE PLAN

Comments ▼

Grade ▼

O = Outstanding
E = Excellent
S = Satisfactory
I = Improving
N = Needs work

Date ▶

Goal	Day 1	2	3	4	5	6	7	Total	Parent Signature

Grade	Technique/Theory	Practice Goals

Grade	Repertoire	Practice Goals

FF1024

PRACTICE PLAN

Comments ▼

Grade ▼

O = Outstanding
E = Excellent
S = Satisfactory
I = Improving
N = Needs work

Date ▶

Goal	Day 1	2	3	4	5	6	7	Total	Parent Signature

Grade	Technique/Theory	Practice Goals

Grade	Repertoire	Practice Goals

FF1024

PRACTICE PLAN

Comments ▼

Grade ▼

O = Outstanding
E = Excellent
S = Satisfactory
I = Improving
N = Needs work

Date ▶

Goal	Day 1	2	3	4	5	6	7	Total	Parent Signature

Grade	Technique/Theory	Practice Goals

Grade	Repertoire	Practice Goals

PRACTICE PLAN

Comments ▼

Grade ▼

O = Outstanding
E = Excellent
S = Satisfactory
I = Improving
N = Needs work

Date ▶

Goal	Day 1	2	3	4	5	6	7	Total	Parent Signature

Grade	Technique/Theory	Practice Goals

Grade	Repertoire	Practice Goals

FF1024

PRACTICE PLAN

Comments ▼

Grade ▼

Date ▶

Goal	Day 1	2	3	4	5	6	7	Total	Parent Signature

Grade	Technique/Theory	Practice Goals

Grade	Repertoire	Practice Goals

FF1024

PRACTICE PLAN

Comments ▼

Grade ▼

O = Outstanding
E = Excellent
S = Satisfactory
I = Improving
N = Needs work

Date ▶

Goal	Day 1	2	3	4	5	6	7	Total	Parent Signature

Grade	Technique/Theory	Practice Goals

Grade	Repertoire	Practice Goals

FF1024

PRACTICE PLAN

Comments ▼

Grade ▼

Date ▶

Goal	Day 1	2	3	4	5	6	7	Total	Parent Signature

Grade	Technique/Theory	Practice Goals

Grade	Repertoire	Practice Goals

FF1024

PRACTICE PLAN

Comments ▼

Grade ▼

O = Outstanding
E = Excellent
S = Satisfactory
I = Improving
N = Needs work

Date ▶

Goal	Day 1	2	3	4	5	6	7	Total	Parent Signature

Grade	Technique/Theory	Practice Goals

Grade	Repertoire	Practice Goals

FF1024

PRACTICE PLAN

Comments ▼

Grade ▼

O = Outstanding
E = Excellent
S = Satisfactory
I = Improving
N = Needs work

Date ▶

Goal	Day 1	2	3	4	5	6	7	Total	Parent Signature

Grade	Technique/Theory	Practice Goals

Grade	Repertoire	Practice Goals

FF1024

PRACTICE PLAN

Comments ▼

Grade ▼

O = Outstanding
E = Excellent
S = Satisfactory
I = Improving
N = Needs work

Date ▶

Goal	Day 1	2	3	4	5	6	7	Total	Parent Signature

Grade	Technique/Theory	Practice Goals

Grade	Repertoire	Practice Goals

FF1024

PRACTICE PLAN

Comments ▼

Grade ▼

O = Outstanding
E = Excellent
S = Satisfactory
I = Improving
N = Needs work

Date ▶

Goal	Day 1	2	3	4	5	6	7	Total	Parent Signature

Grade	Technique/Theory	Practice Goals

Grade	Repertoire	Practice Goals

FF1024

PRACTICE PLAN

Comments ▼

Grade ▼

O = Outstanding
E = Excellent
S = Satisfactory
I = Improving
N = Needs work

Date ▶

Goal	Day 1	2	3	4	5	6	7	Total	Parent Signature

Grade	Technique/Theory	Practice Goals

Grade	Repertoire	Practice Goals

FF1024

PRACTICE PLAN

Comments ▼

Grade ▼

| O = Outstanding |
| E = Excellent |
| S = Satisfactory |
| I = Improving |
| N = Needs work |

Date ▶

Goal	Day 1	2	3	4	5	6	7	Total	Parent Signature

Grade	Technique/Theory	Practice Goals

Grade	Repertoire	Practice Goals

PRACTICE PLAN

Comments ▼

Grade ▼

Date ▶

Goal	Day 1	2	3	4	5	6	7	Total	Parent Signature

Grade	Technique/Theory	Practice Goals

Grade	Repertoire	Practice Goals

FF1024

PRACTICE PLAN

Comments ▼

Grade ▼

Date ▶

Goal	Day 1	2	3	4	5	6	7	Total	Parent Signature

Grade	Technique/Theory	Practice Goals

Grade	Repertoire	Practice Goals

FF1024

EVENT	LEVEL	FEE	TIME	PIECE	COMPOSER

FF1024

TECHNIQUE

Skill ▼	Key ▼											
FIVE-FINGER PENTASCALES	C	G	F	D	A	E	D♭	A♭	E♭	F♯/G♭	B♭	B
Major												
Minor												
Other												

DIATONIC SCALES	C	G	D	A	E	B	F♯/G♭	D♭	A♭	E♭	B♭	F
Major M.M.:												
Natural minor M.M.:												
Harmonic minor M.M.:												
Melodic minor M.M.:												
Other												

CHORDS	C	G	F	D	A	E	D♭	A♭	E♭	F♯/G♭	B♭	B
Major												
Minor												
Diminished												
Augmented												
Inversions: Major												
Inversions: Minor												
Arpeggios: Major												
Arpeggios: Minor												
Cadences:												

Seventh chords	C	G	D	A	E	B	F♯/G♭	D♭	A♭	E♭	B♭	F
Inversions: 7th chords												
Arpeggios: 7th chords												

Dominant 7	Minor 7	Major 7	Diminished 7	Half-Dim. 7		

Technique Books / Etudes / Exercises

REPERTOIRE

Composer ▼	Title/Book ▼	Date Completed ▼	Date Memorized ▼